dear mom,
fuck you

an open letter, in poetry

BETHANY-KRIS writing as
kristen bethany

Copyright © 2024 Kristen Bethany Fournier/Bethany-Kris

All rights reserved.

No reproducing, copying, or distribution of this work is permitted except for small excerpts in reviews.

NOTE: this is not a work of fiction, not a product of the author's imagination, and not the author's falsified experience. Names have and have not been changed.

www.bethanykris.com

ISBN: 9798327261075

For myself.
Because quite frankly, I wrote this one for me.

contents

open letter 1

    dear mom.. 5
    mother wound 7
    yours/mine 9
    love/hate 11
    not mine 13
    poor little you 15
    speak 17
    hilton suite 19
    your daughter 21
    "swim" 23
    only in death 25
    hug 27
    used 29
    war 31
    not sorry 33
    bullets 35
    shots fired 37
    the choice 39
    more years than I haven't 41
    no love lost 43
    hatred 45

the narrative 47

13	51
I once daydreamed books	53
c-ptsd	55
Dicky Fooley	57
I once daydreamed … (part 2)	59
the truth	61
things I miss	63
motherless kid	65
lies	67
12/17	69
Hot Lips	71
maynard	73
do you remember	75
power play	77
trouble	79
can't remember	81
merry-go-round	83
stranger	85
bed of a truck	87

family 89

young	93
kirra	95
my mother's face	97
four	99
siblings	101
cream of mushroom soup	103
how it has to be	105
i win	107
mimi	109
safe	111

anger

mental illness

therapy ... 113

- dragon ... 117
- depression ... 119
- journaling ... 121
- derealization ... 123
- alternatively ... 125
- journaling (part 2) ... 127
- the problem ... 129
- afloat ... 131
- co-dependent ... 133
- cigarettes and rage ... 135
- the monster ... 137
- mommy ... 139
- self-sabotage ... 141

goodbye ... 143

- justify ... 147
- didn't ... 149
- (to the girl I never met) ... 151
- unconditionally ... 153
- still the same ... 155
- nothing ... 157
- do i let you in? ... 159
- closure ... 161
- exceptional ... 163

at the end of the day 165
if i cared to dream 167
forever 169

open letter

welcome to my masterpiece
this pain
it's art
my agony

dear mom

Dear Mom,
I want you to know
before I begin
these words are no haven
from my hands
they're the weapon.

Dear Mom, I once thought
someday we'd see
how these twenty years of silence
could be the answer from me
but I grasp tighter to grudges
than a tattered raft at sea
and letting this go
was un-fucking-likely.

Dear Mom, I'm sorry
let me try again
to explain a better reason
for spilling ink from this pen
listen,
nothing you say
will ever matter
like doing the work
to fix these fractures
those pieces you left
they're still sharp
still shattered
with bloodied, sore hands
always raw
forever shaking
I held it together
this mess of your making.

Dear Mom, it's okay
but tread very lightly
left bare on these pages
well, it's something unsightly
see, she lives within me
and she never died inside you
a demon between us
clinging to truth
a lost, broken girl
neglected and used
screaming her loudest:

Dear Mom,
fuck you.

mother wound

i know the mother wound
intimately
she cut it into you
and then you cut it into me
an undeserved injury
worn unhealed on our sleeve
it's unbearable, visibly

memories haunt your waking dreams
hate that brings us to our knees
pain from which you can never be free

i know the mother wound
intimately

yours/mine

where does the shame
start and end
with the one who knew better
or the one who didn't?

this shame we've inherited
worn like a cloak
heavy on our shoulders
choking at our throats

I once had to carry
your shame and mine
it started with secrets
and we hid those with lies

you've never thought once
how wrong you were
to just carry on living
not healing her

I let you do that, mom, every time
do you hear her screaming now,
deep inside:

whose shame is this, yours or mine?

love/hate

do you still hate the person staring back in the mirror?

well, I hated her, too
for being there

hated so much that she wasn't enough

that she loved
and hated herself
far more than us.

not mine

I often don't like the woman
looking back from the mirror
she stares, contemplating
I see you in her

we're not alike at all

yet…

somehow, we're the same

both changed by your trauma
barely existing
sharing shame

I know it's awful
how it sounds to say:
I'll always hate my mom
but to speak the truth
with you
I'm a shaky, speckled fawn
I'll never be that weak again
not for you
not for anyone

but this poison you left here
well, it kills me a day at a time
so here, I'll give it back now
grasp your last goodbye
hold tight to it and run
run far, run wide
cling to your victimhood
to your side, to your lies

know that no matter what
I will thrive where you have died
take back your slow death
live with it
it's no longer mine

poor little you

poor little you
barely fifteen
won't stay in foster homes
they can't do a thing

poor little you
running the roads
anything to stay away
so you don't go back home

poor little you
not yet a woman
when he touched you like that
when he did what he shouldn't

poor little you
found ways to cope
when mommy didn't care
when you had no hope

then poor little you
chose to make me
a baby at sixteen, but hey
at least you were free

speak

let me tell you something,
not that it will matter.
my mind is a warzone
from which my body can't recover.

it wasn't all bad, i'm sure you'd say. *we had good moments, didn't we? didn't we have good days?*

what good will thinking
of those times make?

all this trauma
clouds my thoughts
and i just hate, hate, hate.

and i barely get a breath
free without you.
you're etched into my bones,
carved into sinew.

why should moments
when you weren't mad,
make me anything
except for sad?
why would i cry
over the scarce
and the few?
those very rare times
when your pain
didn't leave us
black and blue?

the sad part is

i would relive those times
before you wove
your wounds with mine.

before i knew
no one cared
about angry little me
with lice in my hair.

back when i believed
you didn't have a choice.
and then i figured out
only you could have a voice.

hilton suite

Do you remember the Hilton suite?

The man in a three-piece ready to meet?

A sparkly denim thing he bought just for me?

You doing whatever you had to, to please?

Do
you
remember
the
Hilton
suite?

your daughter

i'm the daughter
born from the chaos
of a sixteen-year-old girl
already broken
a bit twisted
from her own little world
with a mother who knew only
how to manipulate
and a stepfather who
got what he wanted
either way

i'm the daughter
of a teenage runaway
who my daddy hid out
so she might stay

i'm the daughter
of a young woman
who couldn't cope
she smoked her lungs
and filled her nose
full of dope
who treated us
with hurtful words
and violent hands
who never once said
she wouldn't do it again

i'm the daughter
of a mother
who doesn't think
she was wrong
but shit, mom
isn't twenty years
terribly long?

"swim"

how little was i
maybe two years grown
you threw me in the river
told me to go
thought it was funny
you and your friends
not even one of them
cared to jump in
how long did i struggle
who really knows
the one boy to save me
you thought him so low
but a toddler in diapers
can't really swim
in a river with currents
where you threw me in

only in death

i promise
the next time i speak to you
will be at a grave
six feet of dirt between us
and me ready to cave

finally able to say
all that i wouldn't
finally able to forgive
all that you couldn't

i need the safety net
only death can provide
a hole where this pain i carry
deep inside
can no longer live
and will ultimately die

it's sad that i still kind of hope
you might die alone
maybe then you could understand
this mess you won't own

hug

you self-medicated
with sex and drugs
desperate to fill
the void that was dug
and i was unfortunately
left to hug
the children you apparently
never loved

used

"she's my firstborn child."

and look what you did.

"don't take her from me."

so he never did.

"she always comes back to me."

but, mom, i didn't

the truth is
these things
never mattered to you
they were just
manipulation
for you
to use.

war

how dare you
speak of me
to anyone
about anything
I gave you
the dignity
of silence
and peace
and anonymity.

but you felt safe
to speak of me
when I stayed quiet
respectfully.

"so you're not coming home?"
"no, I'm not."

and that should have fucking been enough.

I hated you
and you hated me
for every-
fucking-
little-
thing.

I could have gone
another twenty years
never choosing
to face these fears
an abused child's
choice of silence
is the safest place
from rage
and violence.

but you chose war
when you spoke
of me
and made yourself
a victim,
please.

don't confuse our similarities
we're not all the same
you and me
your war of physicality
versus mine
of pure humility,
honestly?

Mother,
never again lie about me.

not sorry

life with you was poverty
lice-filled hair
a travesty
christmases from charity

a total fucking tragedy

weed drying on the ceiling
apartments we were always leaving
men who felt so sleazy
life with you was demeaning

and i *won't* apologize for fleeing

bullets

finding understanding doesn't mean friends
but i always knew why
you picked drugs
rages
and unfortunate men

you never loved yourself enough
so picking them over us
because at least with them
you liked you
while we were just the weapons you grew
pointing straight back at who?

mom
it's you

shots fired

a little girl
sad
tired
and blue
she hurts herself
and
it
hurts you
but all this
you
taught
you rue
i see it
as
what
you're due

the choice

love is a choice
we choose to make
over and over
heart at stake
one of the few
decisions we make
of free will
without needing to take
but your heart was
too full of hate
and now it is
far too late

more years than I haven't

I've been without you
for more years than I haven't
which should make you
completely irrelevant
memory after memory is
horrifying and abhorrent
so this is simply
an acknowledgement
of how I've lived without you
for more years
than I haven't.

no love lost

there's a fine line between here and there
and i know it's hard to hear i don't care
no one said you would like the truth
but wasn't it you who made me bulletproof?

if you can't bear my cold heart
then by all means—play the part
you've always done it very well
and only a few know your tells

choices like these have high costs
and between us there's no love lost
so while you sit, hope, and wait
i define the wall between love and hate

hatred

the hatred comes from knowing
i can't get back
what you took from me
and how i lack

love and trust
family and faith
your stain on my life
is the worst disgrace

above all else
what hurts the most
is now you're just
a painful ghost

i can't wait for the day
when you're dead and gone
so i can finally stop saying
i hate my mom

the narrative

watch me air out all this laundry

when it smells clean
i put it back on

and finally feel seen

13

little girl of thirteen
over-exposed
to mommy's pornography
thinks she knows
everything
and makes a pact to lose her
virginity

little girls of thirteen
don't really know
anything

I once daydreamed books

I once daydreamed books into reality
taking pictures from mind's eye
white paper; black ink
word's silver screen.

I once daydreamed books
could take me away

but it just put me in a corner
hit me harder
and told me to stay.

I once daydreamed to leave it
far in the past

my mother
this pain
that fog never lasts.

I once daydreamed books
it's called dissociation

a skill well-learned
by abused generations.

See,
I'm doing it now
making this poem about you.

So,
I won't have to finish it
telling the whole truth.

I once daydreamed books
into reality

then I figured out the trick
and somehow lost the key.

I still wish that words could take me away
put me in a corner
make me happy there
and then tell me to stay.

I can't daydream books
back to reality

it takes me places
leaves me there
where I don't want to be.

Now when I put
words on the page
I'm present in every sentence
in every possible way.

I don't daydream books
into reality

I don't know how to do it
and continue to breathe.

c-ptsd

so here i am now, mom
thirty-four years old
smoking two packs a day
with a heart that's gone cold

i'll probably hate you forever, mom
that's what i really need to say
hate how you shaped my whole damn life
how my c-ptsd is here to stay

i hope you think about me, mom
far more than i ever did you
hope you know that i did better and more
i hope it haunts you through and through

i learned to live without you, mom
it was hard but i bloomed
in poisoned soil, fed your rotten water
i still grew and grew and grew

eat your fucking heart out, mom
while i pour rage upon this page
show my talent honed from pain you gave me
and allow you one last grace

in a way we're the same, mom
a sad and blatant truth
when you know different you do different
so i chose me and you chose you

Dicky Fooley

you seemed to like married men
and he was just
one of them
but he got a sick kick
in torturing
your neglected kids
force-feeding me
as punishment
food I couldn't fucking stand
you and he
used cocaine
and raped a girl
across the way
then a rotten pizza came
and made us all sick for days
he invited me into bed
"rub my stomach for a bit, kid."
an old house robe
you know it
his erection beneath
couldn't be missed
I can still feel how fast I ran
knowing Dicky was a bad man
I hear him in the recesses
laughing loudly
like he can
that laughter, fuck
still chases me
and what'd you do, mom
sent him to see
twenty bucks
a jawbreaker in hand

"happy birthday"
said that man
"sweet sixteen"
did you not understand
how much I fucking
hated that man
you and me
didn't speak again
after that day
"sorry for all the liver
we made you eat"
but what about the robe
on semen-stained sheets?

and you had the nerve
to say you didn't believe
fuck you, mom
now you'll never be free

I once daydreamed ... (part 2)

My mind's the better place to be
full of dialogues and movie screens
sometimes I even forget to breathe...

you see
I had to
find that
place

avoid all slaps with a stone-like face.

have you ever felt the terror begin
as your mother rages again?

"was that a fucking dirty look"
careful of her mean right hook

she doesn't care, kid
she's not your friend
you think it matters and
she even hits her men

"you little bitch"
"I hate you"

And I can't stand these fucking rooms
of thinking why she's locked me in
burdened and carrying all her sins.

Now she fucks another down the hall
and you're the babysitter
a house slave
doing it all

drugs and rages every night
I hope you see
why my fight

my mind's the better place to be
anything but reality.

a childhood somehow survived
and PS—Mom
I hoped you'd die

the truth

i got caught smoking
at twelve years old
but it started at ten
don't you know
stealing tubes
on the go
and using pencils
to roll tobacco

at Steve's place
tucked under the bed
i kept it all
well-hidden
just to make
a few cool friends

one of many
lies you told
is how you caught me
smoking
at twelve years old
and of course, i then left home

bitch, don't
this is why you're all alone
a liar with no backbone
and a mother i have disowned

it's not the reason i chose to soar
you caught me a year before

things I miss

I miss the way I once looked at my pen
the words never stopped
the stories had no end
I miss the times I can't get back
the old days before life
came to color me in black
when I couldn't imagine
a life being older
and the years going by
didn't turn me colder
I miss the people who were gone in a flash
I can't get them back
and it left me to crash
I miss when my boys were little and sweet
dimpled hands, tiny feet
and dirt-speckled cheeks
I miss that time between living and growth
and I was too stupid to know
about life's chokehold
it took me for a ride
and didn't let go
using my own hands to dig
a grave to call home
a place where I put
the dead part of me
see, she cared too much once
and it just left her to bleed

but I can't miss the mom I didn't have and never knew

I got what I got
and that was you

motherless kid

a child should have a mother
filled of love and touched by fate
instead i got a mother
fueled by rage and kissed by hate
a mother who thought
screaming and hitting
fixed it all
who had no problem
putting heads through walls

i should have had a mother
who showed kindness and grace
an example for an angry child
of the first safe space

but, no
my mother knew only
what she had been taught
by a bad mother of her own
with little thought

no emotional regulation
just an abomination
bodily desecration
and more manipulation

i wish i'd had a mother
who loved me even a bit
but then i figured
with you
it was easier
to be a motherless kid

lies

mommy liked to say
you had your daddy's eyes
but like everything else
this was also a lie

12/17

i was twelve
he was seventeen
i was piss and vinegar
but not yet mean
thought i knew damn well everything
but people like that
you know nothing

i never understood
why she left us be
with a boy
a babysitter his age, i mean
one would think her history
might throw a red flag
even she could see

but no
oh, no
little darling
she was far too selfish to be worrying
in a ground floor apartment
of a high rise building
on an old, ratty couch
while the siblings were sleeping
i was twelve
he was seventeen
and he thought he could touch me

he was cute
tall
and blond, or so i remember
i was boy-obsessed

but not yet a teenager
thought i knew what we were doing
his game of chicken-or-go seemed silly
but even when i said chicken and not go
he kept groping

and groping
and groping

i was barely twelve
he was seventeen

and now you might be wondering
what mommy was doing
oh, partying
at the bar with the angels
or the mall with the teens
twenty-eight and still playing
games
with emotions
of people half her age
she never asked if i was okay
she only got mad
see, doing chores
i wiped the counter
soaked her joint
that she'd use to pay the boy

she can say all she wants:
i don't remember these things
but i do
very well
he was seventeen
and I was twelve

Hot Lips

Hot Lips
mommy's trick
to keep herself on top of it
'cause now she's got a sneaky kid
who lies to get away with shit

or really
to keep from being punished

Hot lips
are mommy's trick
but you learn fast
don't you, kid

if she sends you with ninety-nine
then you come back with thirty-five
steal two and eat them quick
it worked
for a little bit
but

Hot Lips
were just mommy's trick
another excuse
to hit her kid

maynard

My mom was just a girl
when Maynard came into her room.
I'll use the bastard's real name
because he was convicted of this, too.

On little girl bedding,
three sisters slept.
And in he would creep,
straight to their beds.
They prayed every night
for him to choose somebody else.
But either way they listened
as he used a child to please himself.

As my mother got older,
Maynard's methods changed.
To keep her compliant,
he plied her with cocaine.
Abortion after abortion,
they paid them all away.
And my mother's mother had,
well, nothing much to say.

"So what?" she said. *"Should I cry for you? Why should I care?
My brothers did it to me, too."*

Maynard made my mother sick,
but it wasn't him who raged
and it wasn't him who hit.

That's what she
doesn't seem to get.

If only she could comprehend...
what you did to us
was done by your hand.

do you remember

do you remember
driving that fork
into his back
over and over
leaving marks
just like tacks

i don't even know why
you were so mad
just that
forced liver feedings
wouldn't come back

power play

babies were the power play
my mother used to get her way
three babies by three different men
each a pawn
moved at her whim
none of us truly know
how deep her lies go
and grow
weaving through our lives like vines
this tangled mess i now call mine

trouble

"that right there is nothing but trouble."
pappy warned of a girl
she turned their world
to rubble

she was young
and pretty
a little thing, too
an 80s girl
through and through

but he saw the devil
peeking out of you

your trouble came
in every way
and ended with
a glass ashtray
thrown straight at
my father's head

i heard he shared
your sister's bed

can't remember

i never had privacy
or dignity
or a peaceful sleep
with you i just got screaming
and way too much fighting
mental and physical injury

and if that's how you treated thirteen-year-old me…

i'm worried for the toddler and baby
i can't remember ever being

but that's just trauma protecting
these unending feelings
and my brain that's not done filing
away the horror you seemed to be

merry-go-round

weed
pills
cocaine
booze
mommy couldn't seem to choose

but her drug of choice
went up her nose
have you ever seen
the cost of blow?

the men she loved the most, you see
bought it for her, faithfully

while us kids went without
mommy went on another bout

her relationships didn't last
and rock bottom
comes up fast

so who do you think
picked up the pieces?
this merry-go-round
it never ceases

stranger

you're naked
and passed out on the floor again
I don't know that strange man
where he's sleeping next to you
in the fucking living-room

there are kids here I need to feed
and we've got school, eventually
porn still plays on the TV
and later you'll wonder
why I chose to leave

bed of a truck

baby in a box
in the bed
of a truck
that baby was me
shit out of luck
mommy left me
in that box
on the truck
to go to the riverbank
to get high
and fuck

family

the hardest thing i ever did
was learn to truly love my kids

young

it's hard to realize terribly young
that what you had was not a mom
it makes you see her differently
and all the respect you had just leaves

every ounce of love turns to hate
so you barely make it through the day
lest you exacerbate
her monster to come out and play

it's hard to realize terribly young
that what you had was not a mom
it makes you grow up far too quick
and all you wanted was to be a kid

kirra

baby sister asked me why
i left her there with you to cry
a part of me just wants to die

how should i say
i needed to survive
when baby sister   .
asked me why

my mother's face

i don't have my mother's face
i have my mother's pain and rage

the only things she gave to me
besides life and c-ptsd

four

four little boys
you don't know
four lived lies
you didn't grow
four left untouched
your line to toe
four births of mine
you couldn't go
four grandchildren
bear the blow
four beautiful souls
you'll never know

i think what's the worst about all of this
is you will never get to love my kids

they'll never know grammy's kiss
and they'll never know grammy hits

siblings

three of us
came from you
she's bpd's baseline
and he's difficult
too

as for me
on the other hand

i'm sleepless nights
and silent plans
mental illness
ampersands
plotlines
and badlands

choosing creativity
as escape
led me to
a dreamscape

my siblings, though
i think
they just coped…
well,

in their own ways.

cream of mushroom soup

when the cupboards look
a touch forlorn
you go to the dollar store
grab a can of mushroom soup
don't forget the peas, too
add a loaf, pay less than five
'cause we live on the breadline
get home, heat it up
don't forget to add the stuff
pour the slop on toasted bread
this is what you fed your kids

(when you weren't
allowing
a man to
force-feed me things
I didn't like
as punishment—
but at least
we had food,
right?)

how it has to be

i wish i could do what you did
when you saw your mom
in a store with him

"that's a fucking rapist!"

instead
if i saw you
the only thing i would do
is grab my kids and turn to leave
and i would do it
quietly

i've worked too hard for far too long
to protect my kids from all your wrongs
they wouldn't recognize your face
but they know you're not a safe place

all the photos i have of you
i keep tucked away
and quite frankly

i prefer it this way

i am

like a fish without fins
i still learned how to swim
like how a high school diploma for me
was a fanciful whim

like trees without greenery
bend with the wind
adulthood to me
seemed a bad omen

an impossibility
like a fish without fins
then my wedding day happened
and felt like my first real win

all these days, you see
i danced on a rim
of a barrier upon which
you could never get in

mimi

you hated what she did for me
and how i loved her infinitely
she had a knack to save the day
like when i finally ran away

or that time
with a cyst on my thigh
she wouldn't let you
off with your lies

how about when you burned my skin
a cigarette coal, you said back then

and that wasn't even the first one

admit it
you never
should have
been a
mom

my body still carries these scars
while she was the only open heart

and the day we put her in the ground
a part of me could not be found

safe

i keep my rage
hidden away
locked
barred
within a cage

it's not like yours
it doesn't play
and those i love
deserve to be safe

anger

mental illness

therapy

hateful words
on a tear-stained page
that i'll crumple up
and throw away
is the only place
these feelings are safe

dragon

let me rage about these things
until i'm no longer a broken bird that sings
but rather a dragon whose roar will ring
while i hide my young beneath tattered wings

let me rage about these things

depression

my depression is insurmountable
a mountain so high, unconscionable
it stares back at me from dimmed blue eyes
beneath blankets
where i hide
it's a bloodied scalp picked raw again
and a silence that scares my closest friends
while my husband peeks down the hall
and i sink against a shower stall
there's nothing that'll do the job
of pulling me back from the mob
of which has become my thoughts
a battle i have constantly fought
depression feels like the place i'll die
but i've always been scared of suicide
until i made the first plan
i could see it through, i know i can
depression is telling him i'm not safe
and it takes us to the worst place
so end my life—i never did
i won't do that to my kids
isn't one of me enough
i needn't pass on all this stuff
mom already did that to me
and i can't leave my boys to see
even if the cut is made differently:

in reality
from the mother wound
we all bleed

journaling

i failed to journal
every time
and anger is easier
in prose
with rhyme

i needn't be hurtful
anymore
when stanzas on paper
end it
and close doors

derealization

awake at night
i cannot sleep
i cannot think
i cannot blink

fade away now
don't be scared
i'm not there
i'm barely here

alternatively

it's sad to say
it's easier to hate
than it is to admit
she will never be safe

alternatively,

it's distressing to have to
constantly recall
how you helped me to build
these impossibly high walls

journaling (part 2)

I went home and got my face slapped in

after that therapist let you read
strokes of my pen

and I never bothered to journal again.

I mostly just destroyed it all
any writings from my heart's wall

filling fiction pages
with pieces of me
to still get it out
and process things.

the problem

a childhood lived in survival
lead to a body that can't shut down
a mind stuck in a battlefield
and a face that rarely smiles,
barely frowns.

told i was the problem
one starts to believe it
can't see anything but worst-case scenarios
so i strike first
before they land a hit.

afloat

for every single word i wrote

there are far more stories i haven't told

secrets i continue to hold

while i walk down this winding road

with anxiety clawing at my throat

only verity keeps me afloat

co-dependent

over and over and over again
i sat down
pen
in
hand

hoping i could set free
the bitter, broken
pieces
of
me

but somehow we became friends
quite a turn
of
bad
events

and we're kinda co-dependent
if only it
could
make
sense

cigarettes and rage

i medicate
with cigarettes and rage
i ruminate
on memories and pain

what could have been
will never be
how do i accept the fate
dealt to me?

flick the lighter
inhale again
does the rage
ever end?

the monster

i was already depressed
by nine years old
i remember sitting alone
frost on the window
shut away in my room
only a bare mattress
sitting on the floor
with nothing but my thoughts
hell behind a locked door

sometimes i had
books from school
a love started there
and escape became a tool
that day i only
wrote on the glass
finger as my pen
my heart a dead mass
help, it read
written backwards
but nobody ever did
instead
i lost myself in the blizzard

depression is now
my constant friend
chewing at my back
chasing to no end
i know that monster
better than I know myself
there is no relief
there is no help

all because mom hated
how i wouldn't bend
despised how i wouldn't
even pretend

you see, mom
from a terribly young age
i always knew
respect had to be earned
you were no better than me
and you couldn't stand the truth

mommy

mind alight
body tight
fists clenched
ready to fight

i already know
in my head
my path out
while you'll be dead

that's the harsh
reality
of my
c-ptsd

it took years
working on me
to get my mind
to will peace
and ease

i remind
myself
i'm not with
mommy

self-sabotage

is it you or is it me
i cannot eat
sleep
breathe

i still feel your energy
surrounding
pounding
drowning me

was it you
or was it me
who caused these
catastrophes
making up
who i didn't think i'd be

anxiety
rage
they ruin me

i pick my skin until i bleed
a habit learned confined, you see
it infected my mind

like starving, too

all of it, unhealthy

goodbye

the things that make my mother and i the same

are:

bipolar, the mother wound, our blood and the shame

justify

"what was done to me was far worse than what I did to you."

this was the excuse
my mother used

when confronted with
her abuse.

(*and then she said she couldn't remember*)

didn't

it's impossible to decide what's worse—

being the mother who should've
but didn't
believe her kid for even
a minute

or a woman who runs around and says:

"i can't believe my mother treated me this way!"

oh, wait…

you're one in the same.

(to the girl I never met)

i hate to say i wonder about you often,
but i do.

who would you be without all the rest?

maybe that's my real problem.

i focus too much on what i could've done
and leave behind what i've managed to accomplish.

unconditionally

if there were nine hells
i'd walk them all
to never hear
your name be called

i'd dig my heart out
and watch it beat
to never share
the air you breathe

i'd spoon out my eyes
and stab my ears
to never know
that you were here

it's regrettably true
that all of these
are nothing more
than fantasies

you're the person who
gave birth to me
but i still hate you
unconditionally

still the same

as i understand
you've not changed a bit
you still show emotions
with fists that hit
you still like to rage
to fit
to fight
you just changed the drugs
you do at night

the years took away
what made things easy
who sees bad
in something pretty?

but now you're just
broken art
alive and living
with a broken heart

when asked i say:
it's what she deserves

ugly and alone
karma served

nothing

i think people
expect me to say
that i'll somehow
forgive away
all the things
you did to me
as if forgiveness
is the key
but every promise
you ever made
was another means
to get your way
and i already
forgave you
knowing the whole
sordid truth
what forgiveness
taught me
is that
i'm too good
at lying
for anger like mine
it seems
forgiveness did
nothing

do i let you in?

i should have been able to be the girl
making her way into the world
by learning herself through every mistake
and finding growth in the heartache

but the thing that i misunderstood
was i never had a girlhood
the younger me couldn't thrive
consumed with needing to survive

but that part of me never died
instead i gave her a place to hide
deep inside a heart that froze
where only those i love can go

closure

i write myself
late into the night
and let the pain
inside
take flight
the only way
i know to fight
is to let this flame
i hold
burn bright
let it consume me
to the core
until i'm only
ash on a floor
smoldering forevermore
can't you see why
i must close this door?

exceptional

I am the exception
to every rule
I beat statistics
I finished school
I did everything
you couldn't do

what you didn't
or wouldn't
I saw it through.

half of me
is a piece of you
but a part of me
always knew:
I am fucking exceptional

because I am not you.

at the end of the day

what all of this really means to say
is you will never,
ever change

and, mom

i don't want to be the same

if i cared to dream

you're not really a thought
passing my mind
well, maybe
occasionally
from time to time

once in a blue moon
when my soul aches
and the past comes around
to grate and take

if i cared to dream
about me and you
i'd hope in another life
we could be brand new

stripped of memories
of the pain
of violence

our brokenness healed
by space
and silence

but if living without you
taught me anything
it's that i can still fly
with fractured wings

forever

imagine how you got away
with every single fucking thing

while i sit high
on a mountain that cries
from being built up
on your crimes

so my traumas,
i've posterized
and with this
your legacy

is *immortalized.*

goodbye.

author's note

I just want to give a special thanks to a handful of specific people who either were the catalyst to me beginning the journey that became *dear mom, fuck you* or significantly helped me along the way.

Dustin., Ari R., and Lindsay R. and Eli—I love you all, and thank you. Each in your own way, you all know what you've done.

Lee, for the cover, I owe you much gratitude. You did what I couldn't do and it's perfect.

xo,
kristen bethany

about the author

Kristen Bethany is the given name of prolific romance author Bethany-Kris. She's a mother, a Canadian, and a lover of things that are usually bad for her. She used to destroy her poetry, but not anymore.

www.bethanykris.com

Made in the USA
Middletown, DE
01 April 2025